Mel Bay Presents

Rock Gui...
for the Young Beginner

By
Corey
Christiansen

Online Audio

To Access the Online Audio Go To:
www.melbay.com/20148BCDEB

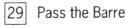

ONLINE AUDIO

1	Tuning	11	Stage Right	21	No More
2	Rollin´ On	12	Stage Left	22	Please Do Not Touch
3	Out of Cash	13	Dude	23	Bob's Jam
4	Dead Gone	14	What ?	24	Blind Panel
5	Baby Child	15	Serious Power	25	Low Riffin´
6	Clean Out	16	Nirvous	26	Barring Low
7	Broken Up	17	Long Gone	27	Barring Around
8	Seperate ways	18	Moveable Blues	28	Sore Digits
9	Solid Ground	19	Moveable Blues II	29	Pass the Barre
10	Voit's Baron	20	Falling Up		

1 2 3 4 5 6 7 8 9 0

Visit us on the Web at www.melbay.com — E-mail us at email@melbay.com

Table Of Contents

Introduction

I started playing guitar fairly young and was soon after drawn to the sounds of rock guitar. At a very young age I loved listening to the recordings of popular rock bands of the time and loved sitting in my room trying to figure out what all of my favorite guitarists were doing to get those great sounds. I'm happy to put out a method that will teach young guitarists the tricks to sounding like their favorite rock artists. The examples in this book will get students started on the right track, but after they get things going they should work through other books and try to "rip" things off recordings to continue their musical journey. This is a starter book that introduces many of the concepts every good rock guitarist in the world is familiar with and provides some "real life" exercises.

Most of all this method is supposed to be fun. The first few pages contain some basic information on playing the guitar in general. The rest of the material is pure rock guitar basics. Be sure to use the play-along CD to help with practicing. While the musical examples are written out quite clearly, it always helps to hear what it's supposed to sound like. Also, playing with the CD will help students learn faster and get the right sound.

Any type of guitar (acoustic or electric) may be used with this method. Rock music uses all types of guitars. However, there are some of the examples on the CD that will use certain electric guitar sounds and effects. If you have those sounds, fantastic, use them when you practice. If you don't have those sounds or effects, no worries; just play the exercises with a clean or even an acoustic guitar sound. They'll still sound great.

Let's get started! It's time to rock out!

Corey

Reading the Music Diagrams

The music in this book will be written using chord diagrams, tablature and standard notation. Here is a quick review.

Chord diagrams will be used to illustrate chords and scales. With the chord diagrams, the vertical lines represent the strings on the guitar, with the first string being on the right. The horizontal lines represent frets, with the first fret being on the top. Dots, or numbers, on the lines show the placement of left-hand fingers. The numbers on, or next to the dots indicate which left-hand finger to use. A diamond may be used to indicate the placement of the root of the chord or scale. **Root** refers to a note which has the same letter name as the chord or scale.

A zero above a string indicates the string is to be played open (no left-hand fingers are pushing on the string). An "X" above a string indicates that string is not to be played, or that the string is to be muted by tilting one of the left-hand fingers and touching the string lightly.

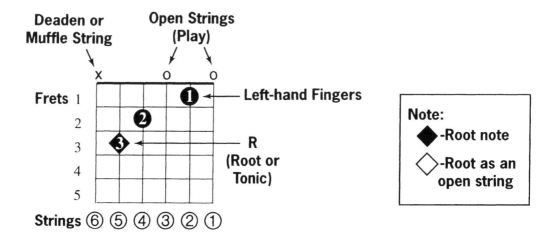

Music Fundamentals

The five lines and four spaces in music is called a **staff**. At the beginning of each line, a treble clef, or G clef, is written on the staff. The treble clef will be discussed later. The staff is divided into sections with **bar lines**. The sections between the bar lines are called **measures**. Inside each measure there are **beats**. Beats are the pulse of the music or measurements of time. The number of beats in each measure can be determined by looking at the **time signature.** The time signature is the fraction which appears at the beginning of the music.

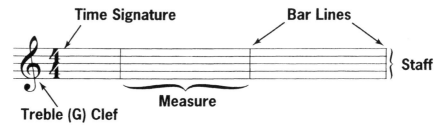

The top number in the time signature indicates the number of beats in each measure. If "C" is written, the piece is in 4/4. C stands for **common time**.

Common Time ($\frac{4}{4}$)

Strum Bars

A **chord** is when three or more strings are played at the same time. Often, when playing chords, the strings are strummed. For the exercises and songs in this book, the chords will be strummed with a pick. When strumming, the right-hand wrist rotates slightly, and the arm moves from the elbow as the pick moves across the strings. When strumming the strings down, be sure to strum straight down. Do not strum outward. Written below are several strum bar signs. Each is a down strum, but the length of the strum varies. The time value of each strum is written to the side. This mark, ⊓, written above the strum bar, indicates a downstroke. If the strum gets more than one beat, strum the strings on the first beat, and allow them to ring for the additional beats. This mark, V, written above the strum bar, indicates an upstroke. Practice playing each strum bar several times while strumming all six strings open. **Open** means that <u>no</u> left-hand fingers are pushing on the strings.

= 1/2 beat

= 1 beat

= 2 beats

= 3 beats

= 4 beats

Tablature

Another way of writing guitar music is called tablature. The six horizontal lines represent the strings on a guitar. The top line is the first string. The other strings are represented by the lines in descending order as shown below.

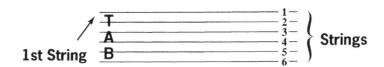

A number on a line indicates in which fret to place a left-hand finger.

Number indicates fret

A number on a line indicates in which fret to place a left-hand finger.

In the example below, the finger would be placed on the first string in the third fret.

1st String, 3rd Fret

If two or more numbers are written on top of one another, play the strings at the same time.

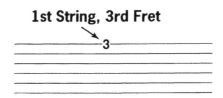

Rhythm Exercises

Below are a number of rhythm exercises. Don't worry about playing a chord or specific note with this exercise. Just play the rhythms strumming any number of open strings. Tapping your foot on the beat (four times in each measure) will help you keep track of when each strum should occur. Also, say the beat number out loud as you strum. This simple exercise will help you develop good time and rhythm which is an important thing for any rock guitarist.

Rock Basic Rhythms

tie: lets the first note/chord ring through the second

Open Chords

Every rock guitarist must know some open chords. Here are some diagrams that show many important open chords.

Major Chords

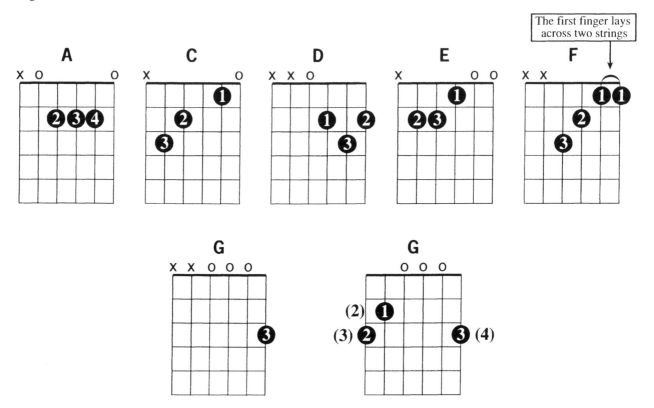

Minor Chords

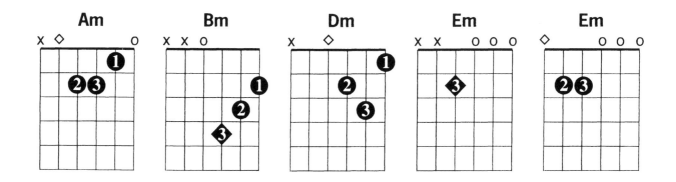

Seventh Chords

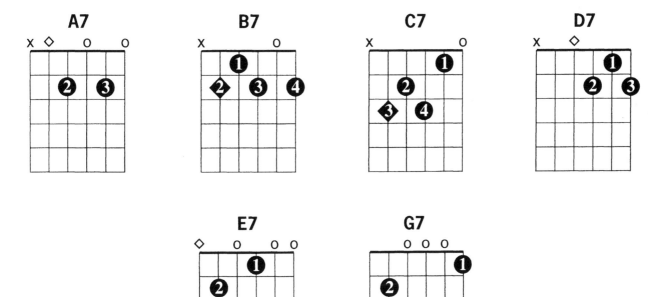

Now that we've got the basics together let's get to some playing. Here are some tunes that use open chords.

CD Track #

Rollin' On

9

Out of Cash

Fast Rock

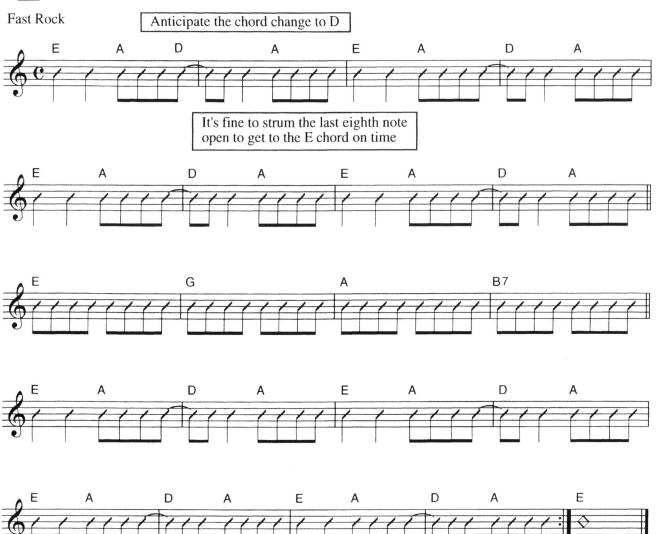

Anticipate the chord change to D

It's fine to strum the last eighth note
open to get to the E chord on time

10

This next tune uses a dead strum (✗). Dead strums are very effective in rhythm rock guitar because they give a percussive sound to the guitar. You make the dead strum by slapping the palm of your right hand against the strings as you strum the chord. No notes should ring through, just the sound of the pick hitting "dead" strings.

Dead Gone

disc Tr. 4

Classic Rock

When there is a measure without a chord name, continue playing the last chord (Em in this case).

Two very popular chords in rock are the add9 (sometimes written with sus2 or just with a 2) and the suspended chord (sometimes written with sus4 or just with a sus). Both of these chords have a great "clean" sound to them.

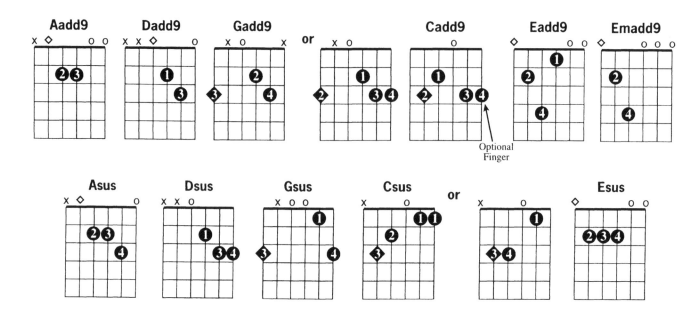

The following tunes use add9 and sus4 chords.

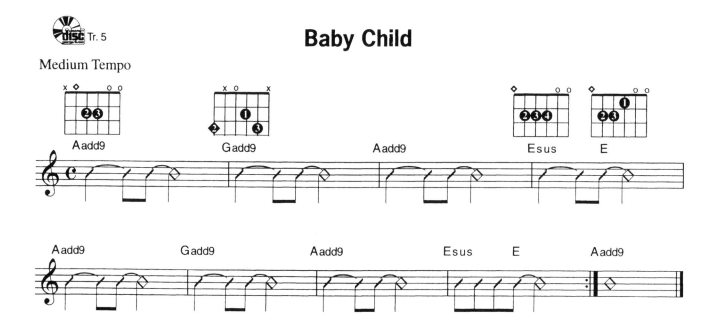

Tr. 5

Baby Child

Medium Tempo

12

Clean Out

Medium (80's Rock)

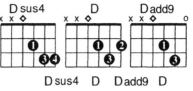

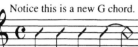

Notice this is a new G chord.

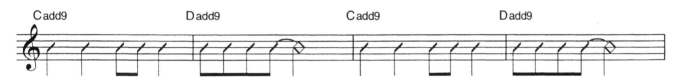

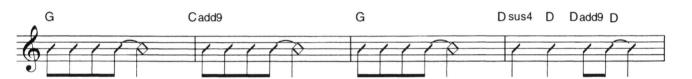

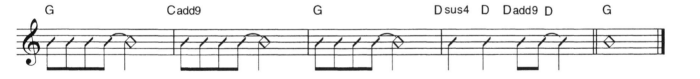

13

Sometimes it sounds cool to break up the chords by picking individual notes rather than strumming. A broken up chord is called an arpeggio. Use the standard notation and tab to read these charts. Have fun with these tunes.

Broken Up

Tr. 7

Rock Ballad

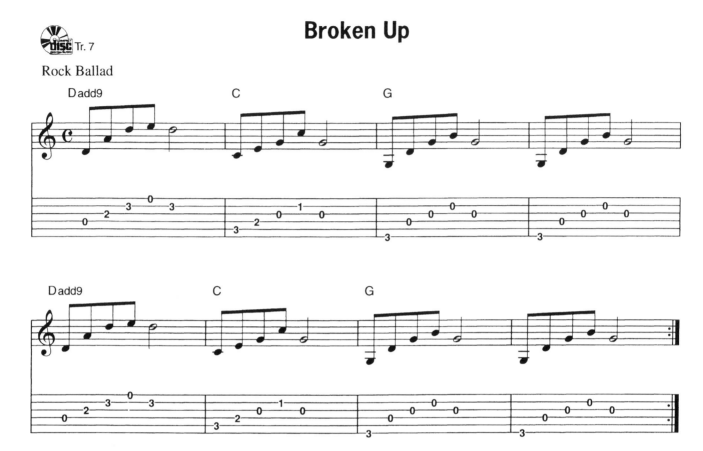

Separate Ways

Tr. 8

Medium Ballad

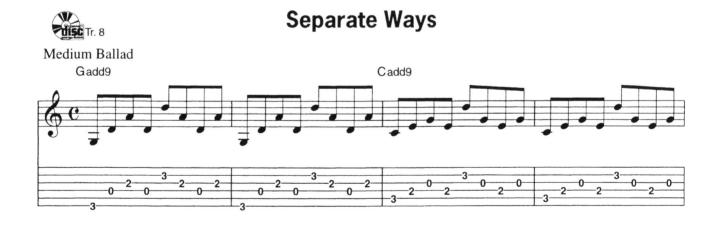

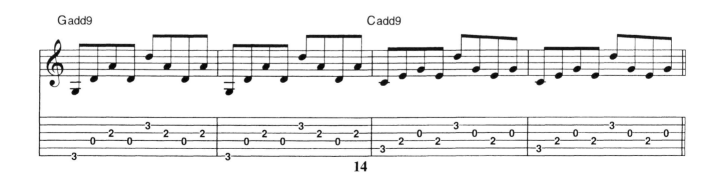

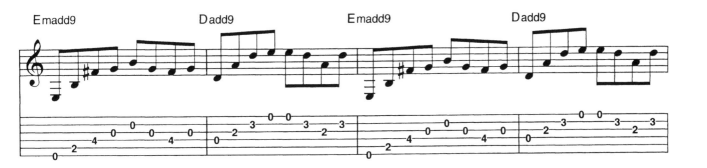

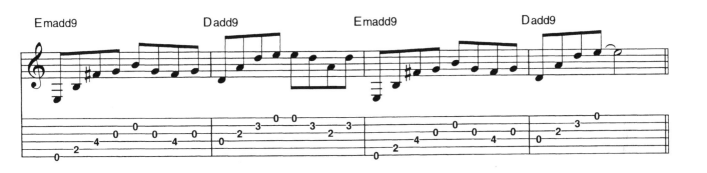

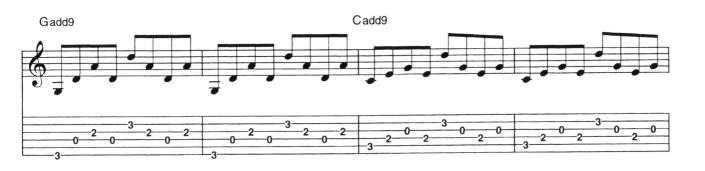

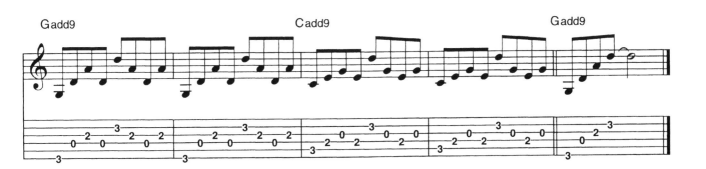

The next few tunes use chords with added bass notes. Usually the lowest note in an open chord is the root (the note that names the chord or scale). For example, a C chord usually has a C note as the lowest note. Chords with added bass notes are sometimes called slash chords. Below are a few common slash chords. These chords usually function as connectors from one chord to another. It's nice to use slash chords to create an interesting bass line within a chord progression.

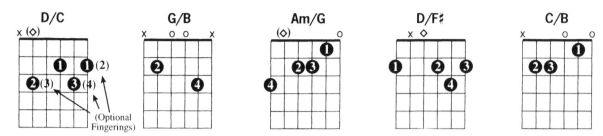

Solid Ground

16

Voit's Baron

Acoustic Rock

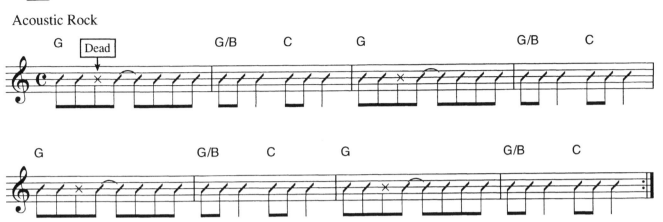

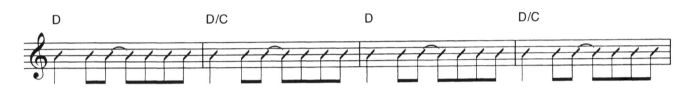

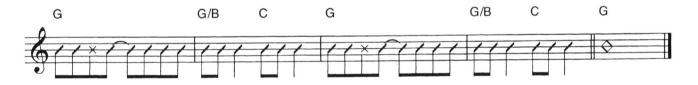

Power Chords

Power chords are one of the most important things a rocker must know. They are the backbone of some of the greatest rock songs in history. They are also called "5" chords. So, E5 or A5 would mean E power chord or A power chord. The diagrams below show three open power chords.

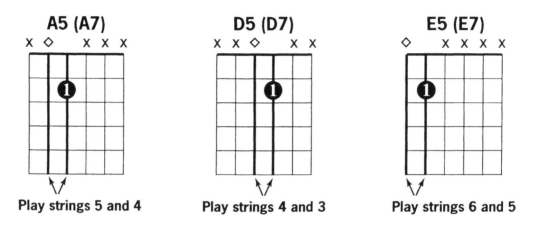

When playing power chords, be sure to pick both notes quickly so they sound simultaneously. Chord diagrams for the A, D, and E open power chords are shown above. In the blues, power chords are often used in place of seventh chords.

Here are a few tunes that use these power chords.

Stage Right

Tr. 11

Driving Rock Groove

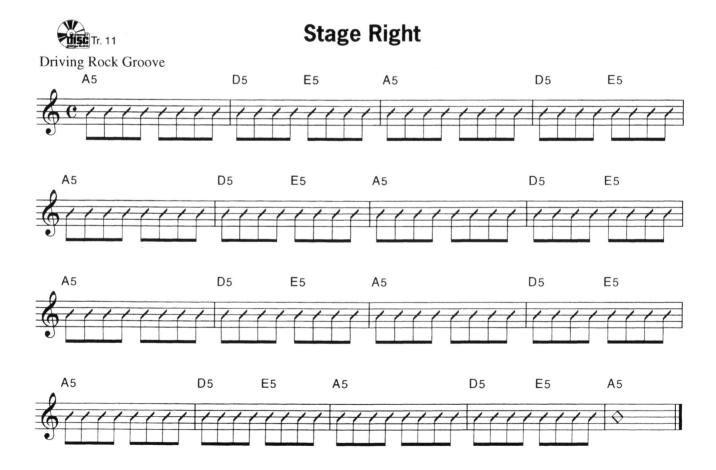

Stage Left

Classic Rock

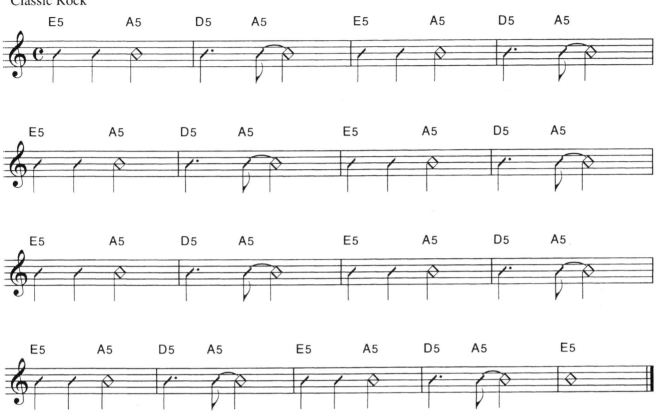

These other sets of power chords are called moveable power chords. The shape of the power chord can be moved anywhere on the fretboard. The lowest note is usually the root. The root is the note that gives the chord its name. There are charts below showing how this works, but basically whatever fret and string the root is on give the power chord its name. The trick is memorizing all of the notes on the 6th and 5th string. It's not really that hard.

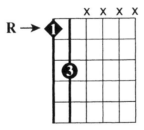

Sixth String Roots

Fret	0	1	3	5	7	8	10	12
Root Name	E	F	G	A	B	C	D	E

19

Moveable power chords may be played on any fret. For example, B5 would have the root on the 6th string on the 7th fret.

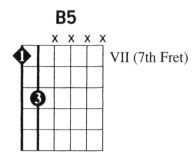

To sharp a power chord, move the pattern up one fret. To flat a power chord, move the pattern down one fret.

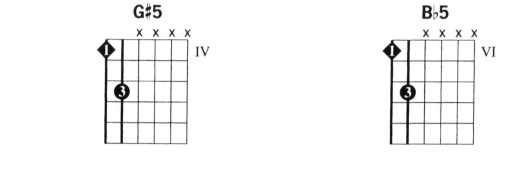

 Tr. 13

Dude

*Use 6th string power chords for this exercise

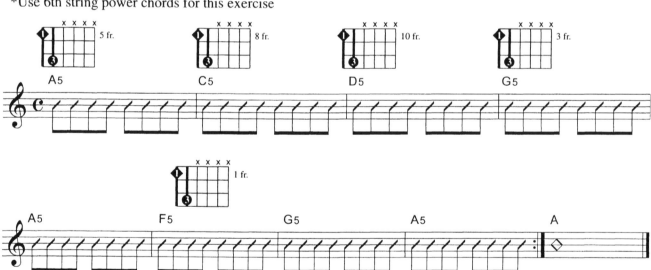

Power chords may also be played with the root on the 5th string. The diagram below shows how this is done. A C5 power chord with the root on the 5th string is positioned so the finger on the 5th string is in the 3rd fret (C).

C5

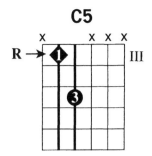

The chart below shows the locations of the note names (roots) on the 5th string.

Fifth String Roots

Fret	0	2	3	5	7	8	10	12
Root Name	A	B	C	D	E	F	G	A

 Tr. 14

What?

*Use 5th string power chords for this exercise

accent mark: strum the chord a bit harder and louder when it appears above a strum bar or note.

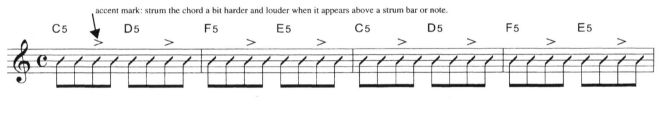

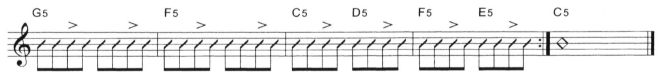

Now let's combine the two categories of power chords to play some classic rock anthems.

  Tr. 15

Serious Power

Heavy Rock

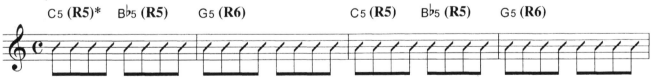

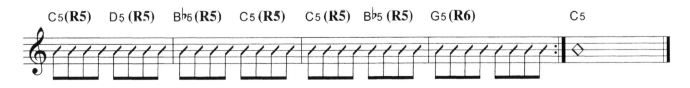

*The R5 or R6 indicates which type of power chord (root on 5th or 6th string) should be used.

Nirvous

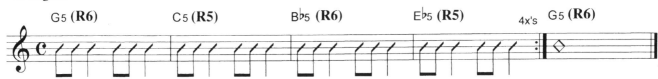

Each student should decide on their own, which category of power chord to use for the next exercises.

Long Gone

Moveable Blues

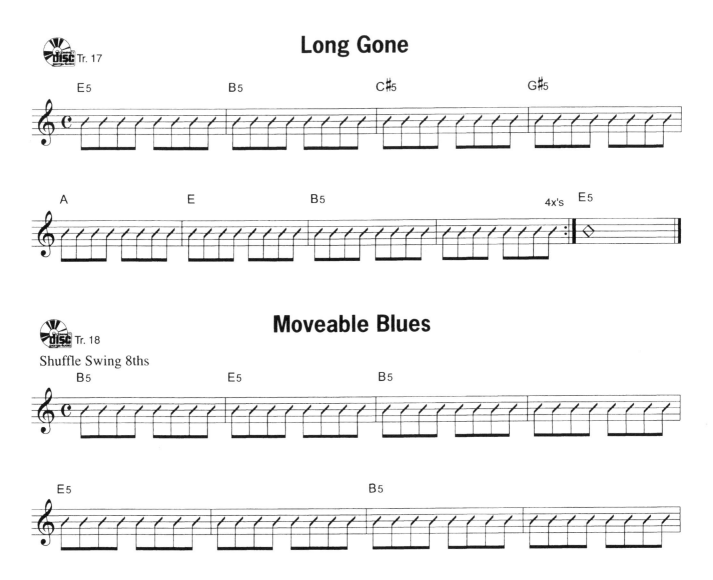

Moveable Blues II

Medium Blues

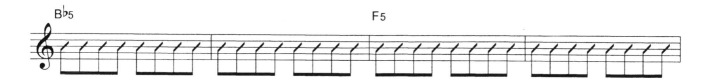

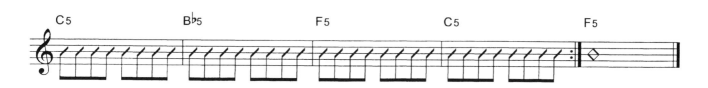

By knowing power chords anyone can write an original rock hit. Here's some blank music paper to get you started. Experiment with power chord combinations that sound good to you and then write the chord names down on this paper. This step will help you remember what you did. If there are any rhythms that are hard to remember, they can be written down as well. Who knows, the material that is written down here could be the next rock classic.

Scales

There are a couple of scales that every rock guitarist must know. The minor pentatonic scale is the Holy Grail of rock scales. It sounds great when played against minor chords or chord progressions in a minor key. The open E and A minor pentatonic scales are shown below.

Open E Minor Pentatonic

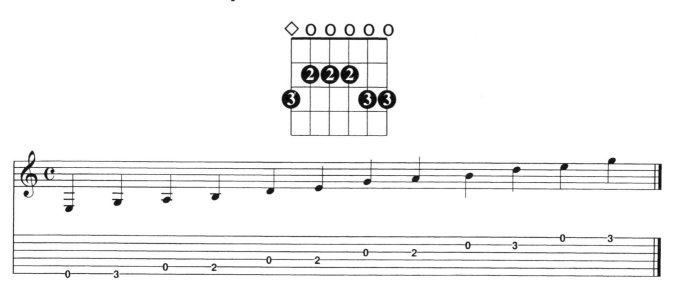

Open A Minor Pentatonic

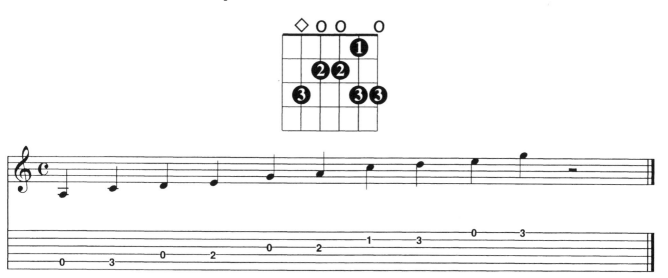

Moveable scale patterns for the 6th string root and the 5th string root are shown on the next page. Moveable scale patterns work the same as moveable chord shapes. Whatever note the root starts on names the scale.

Moveable Minor Pentatonic Scales
Sixth String Roots

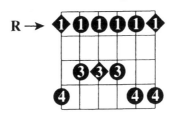

Fret	0	1	3	5	7	8	10	12
Root Name	E	F	G	A	B	C	D	E

Fifth String Roots

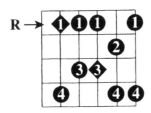

Fret	0	2	3	5	7	8	10	12
Root Name	A	B	C	D	E	F	G	A

To sharp the scale, move the pattern up one fret. For example, the G♯ minor pentatonic scale begins on the 6th string on the fourth fret. To flat the scale, move it down one fret. For example, the B♭ minor pentatonic scale begins on the 6th string on the 6th fret.

Here are some great exercises to get these scales under your fingers. Even though these are just exercises, these groupings of notes sound great in solos. Make sure to try these sequences with the moveable scale patterns as well.

Pentatonic Sequence I

E Minor Pentatonic

*Practice slowy to begin.

Pentatonic Sequence II

E Minor Pentatonic

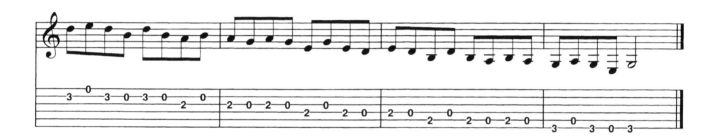

Pentatonic Sequence III

A Minor Pentatonic

Pentatonic Sequence IV

A Minor Pentatonic

Check out these rock solos that use the minor pentatonic scale.

Tr. 20

Falling Up

E Minor Pentatonic

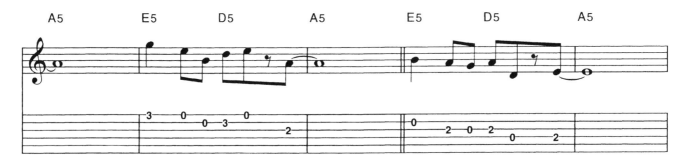

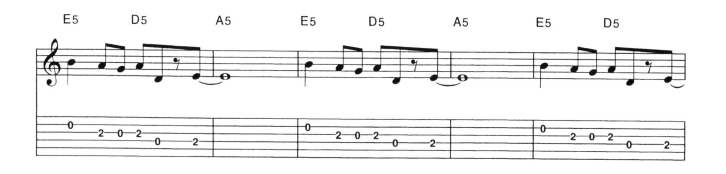
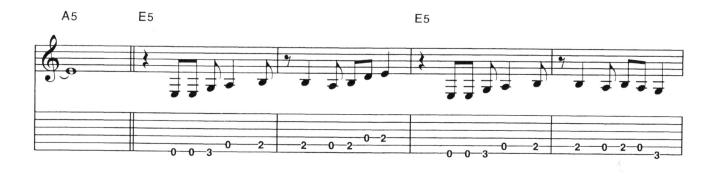

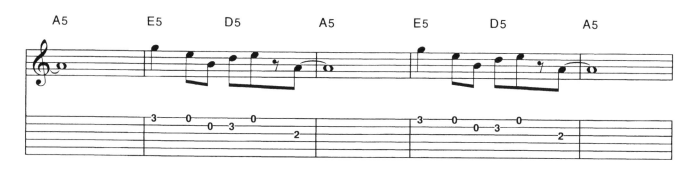
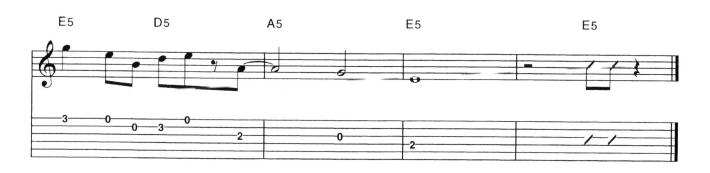

No More

Rhythm Guitar Intro

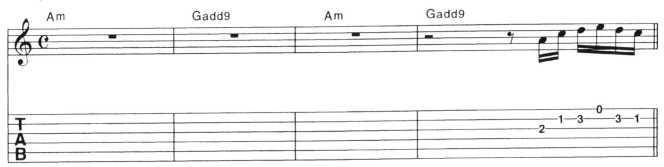

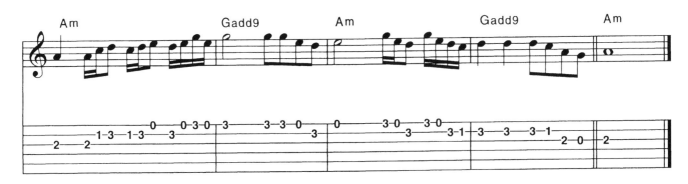

Use the moveable D minor pentatonic scale for this play-along. This would be the 6th string pattern in the 10th fret or the 5th string pattern in the 5th fret.

Tr. 22

Please Do Not Touch
Scale Play-Along #1

High Energy Rock

Use the moveable G minor pentatonic scale. This would be the 6th string pattern in the 3rd fret or the 5th string pattern in the 10th fret.

Tr. 23

Bob's Jam
Scale Play-Along #2

Reggae

One of the coolest sounds is combining power chords with a riff from the scale. Have fun with these.

Blind Panel

Funky

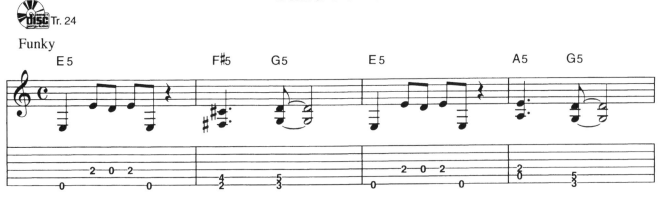

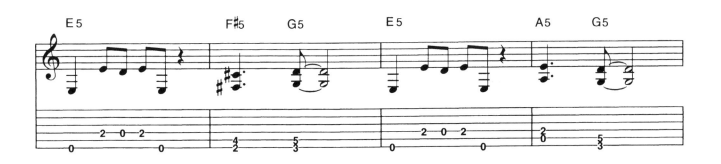

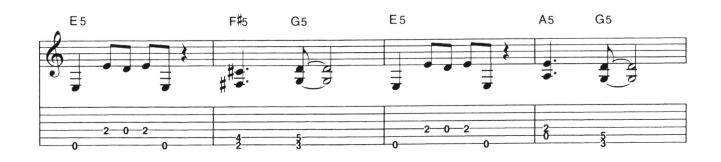

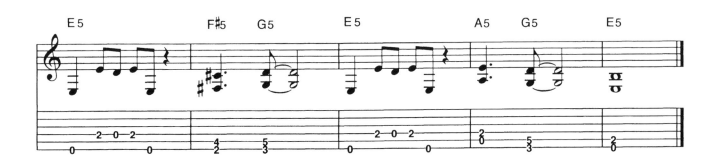

Low Riffin'

Heavy Rock

Barre Chords

Barre chords get their name because two or more notes in the chord are played by laying one finger across multiple strings. They are moveable chords just like the power chords. Here are some common 6th and 5th string barre chords

6th String Rooted Barre chords

Major
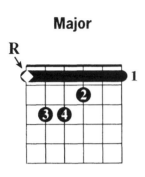

Minor
m
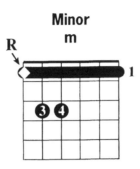

Seventh
7
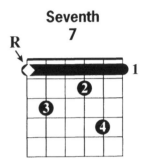

Minor Seventh
m7
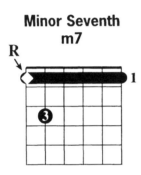

Suspended
sus
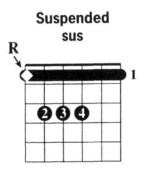

Seventh Suspended
7sus
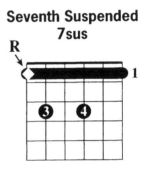

Minor-Major Seventh
m+7
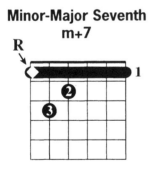

Ninth
9
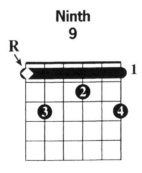

Add Nine
add9
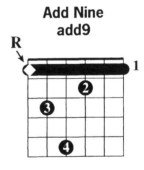

Minor Ninth
m9
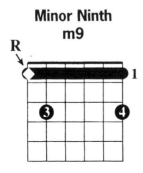

Minor Add Nine
m/9
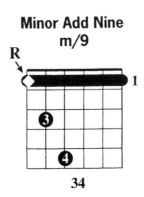

Thirteenth
13
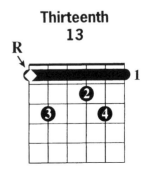

5th String Rooted Barre chords

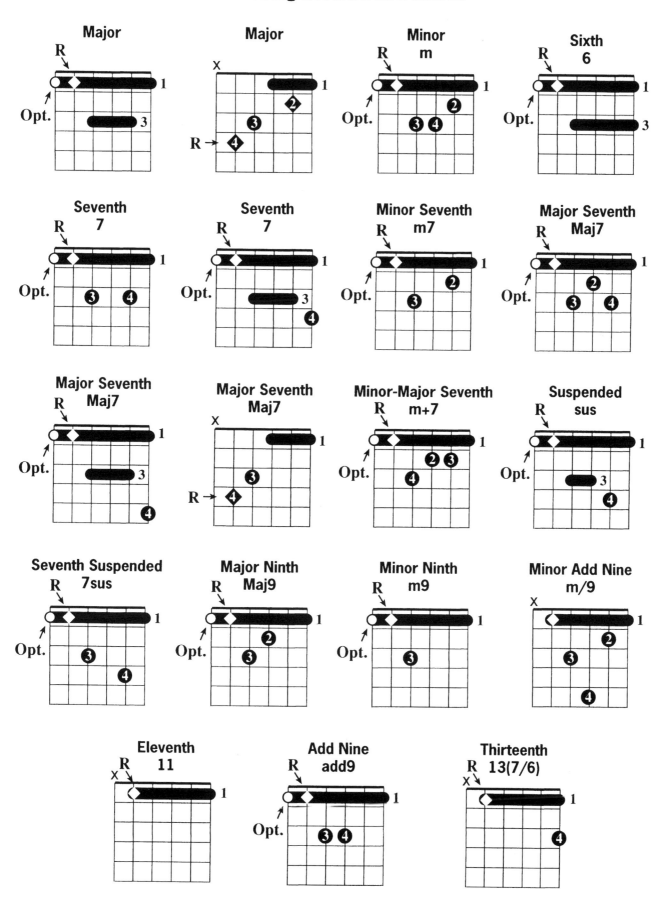

Here are a number of exercises that use barre chords.

These first exercises only use barre chords with roots on the 6th string.

Barring Low

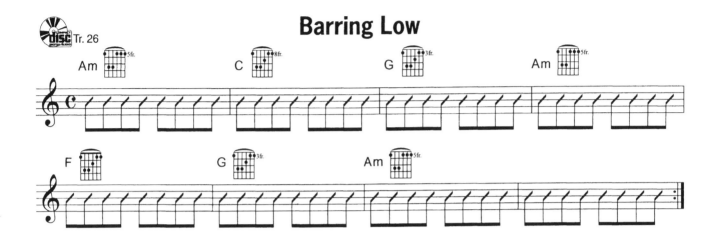

Barring Around

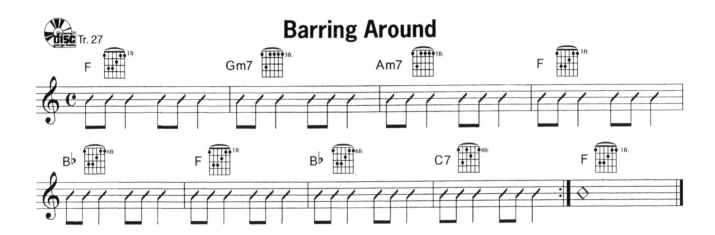

These next exercises only use barre chords with the roots on the 5th string.

Sore Digits

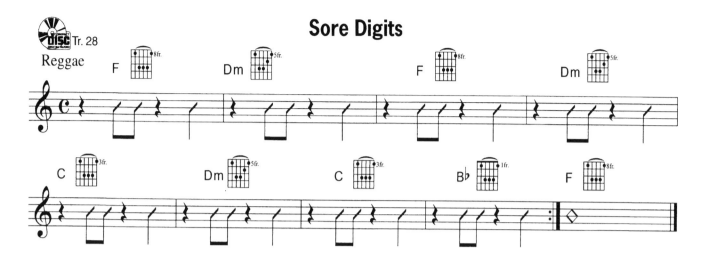

Pass the Barre

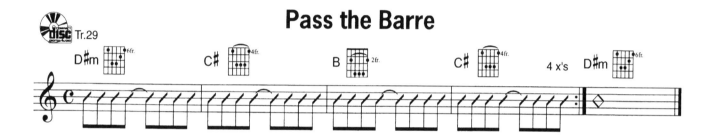

Integration

The following exercises make use of 6th and 5th string rooted barre chords. You decide which category each chord should come from. Keep the fingerings as close together as possible.

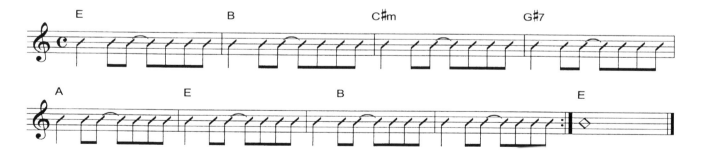

The Arch

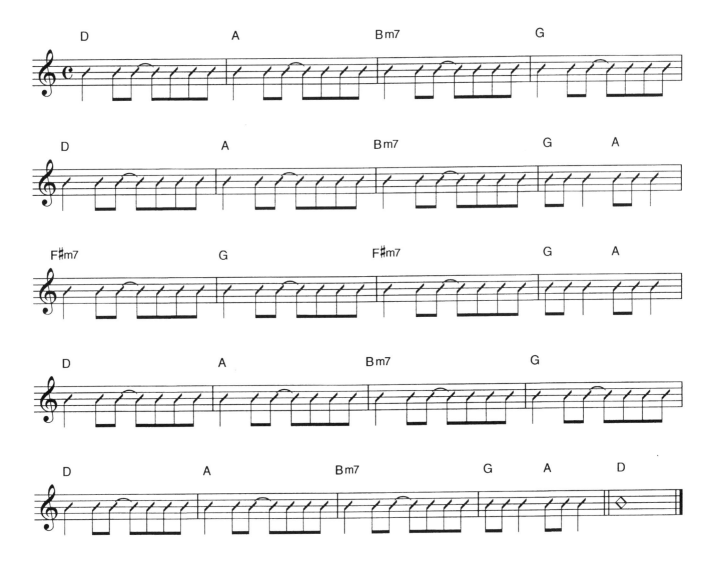

This text has provided a number of techniques and examples as well as some playing opportunities to get you familiar with the essentials of rock guitar. Don't stop now. This is just the beginning. For further study check out some of the many other Mel Bay books on rock guitar. Have fun developing your musical vocabulary.

Corey

Printed in Great Britain
by Amazon

82046867R00025